A FRIEND IN GRIEF

SIMPLE WAYS TO HELP

DEDICATION

To my family, my husband David,
my son Zeb, my brother Wayne,
and my sisters Myra and Dicksey.
I can't imagine my life without you.

And to Sara Jane who lives
in all our hearts.

A FRIEND IN GRIEF

SIMPLE WAYS TO HELP

GINNY CALLAWAY

To lee,
with love,
Ginny Callaway

HIGH WINDY PRESS
PO Box 553
Fairview, NC 28730
www.afriendingrief.com
(800) 637-8679

ISBN # 978-0-942303-49-0
Library of Congress Subject headings
        Grief
        Bereavement

_____

Book and cover design and illustrations by Dana Irwin

www.irwindesigns.com   irwindana@bellsouth.net

Note to the Reader

As you read this book, your own experiences with death and grief may surface. These feelings may be intense and surprising, because grief is one of the most powerful emotions. Allow that pain to help you understand your friend's pain. Use your time to reflect on a loss that you may not have completely processed. Your empathy, compassion and personal experience will support you as you reach out to your friend. Your own healing will continue, too.

Contents

INTRODUCTION
MY STORY

On Monday, November 13, 1989, my children and I moved into our dream house. My husband, David, who is a musician, was on tour in Texas, so the move was in my hands. It was a glorious, sunny day and the movers were as nice and helpful as could be. We were so excited. It had taken us five years to find this house and it was just what we wanted, with room to spread out just as the kids were becoming teenagers. Everything was perfect.

Tuesday was still beautiful. I let the kids stay home from school to unpack their boxes and settle into their rooms. Zeb, 13, helped Sara Jane, 10, in her room for a while, and then Sara Jane helped Zeb with his. I was tickled to see the big brother come out in Zeb, as he advised her where she should place her dollhouse in relation to her bed. Later that afternoon, I went to our old house to pick up Spike, our cat, and take him to the vet to be sure he had no fleas before moving him in, too. I couldn't stop smiling.

As day turned to evening, the sky clouded over. By six o'clock, the thunder and lightning started and the rain began. I drove Zeb to his Boy Scout meeting, then Sara Jane and I returned to have dinner with new neighbors.

Sara Jane at only 10 was so confident. She talked to these adults as if she had always known them, even though she met them for the first time that night. I remember looking at her across the table, seeing a light around her, feeling very proud of her. She charmed everyone.

When we drove to pick up Zeb after dinner, it was raining harder. Since no school bus ran in our new neighborhood, I made plans for another neighbor and good friend, Sandy, to pick Zeb up in the morning and take him to school with her boys. I would drive Sara Jane to her school a little later. Then Sandy and I would meet back at my house to put my kitchen together, which was one big stack of boxes.

Wednesday morning was dismal. The storm was at its worst. The sky was black, and though the clock said 7:30 AM, it looked like the middle of the night outside. I drove Zeb to the bottom of our driveway to meet Sandy, then drove back to the house to pick up Sara Jane and take her to school.

■ I REMEMBER LOOKING AT HER ACROSS THE TABLE, SEEING A LIGHT AROUND HER, FEELING VERY PROUD OF HER

I was really excited about the prospect of getting my kitchen organized, but Sara Jane was being a little slow, worrying about her hair. I got angry saying, "You're going to

be late for school. Don't worry about your hair. Hurry up."
She got upset, and crying softly, gathered up her school things.
With her shoes in hand, she got in the car and sat beside me.

That is the last thing I remember until I woke up in the hospital. Steve, David's best friend, was leaning over me, asking,
"Where's David?" All I could say was Texas. I didn't know
where I was or what was going on.

Later I was told what had happened. On the way to taking
Sara Jane to school, our car had hydroplaned sideways on
a flooded street, right into the path of an oncoming pickup
truck. The truck hit Sara Jane's side of the car just behind
where she was sitting. The car was dented into a "V" shape,
with the "V's" point jutting in right behind Sara Jane's head.
There were no eyewitnesses other than the three men in
the truck we hit. The first person on the scene was a nurse
taking her own child to school. She came to the car and
reached in to help. The nurse somehow got Sara Jane breathing again and stayed with us until the ambulance arrived. It
took the paramedics, firemen and the Jaws of Life over one
hour to get us out of the car. It was still raining so hard that
the Highway Patrol closed the entire road.

The newspaper report said Sara Jane was unconscious and I
was semi-conscious. It also said I was holding her in my arms.
Although I have no memory of the accident, that image, those
words—"holding Sara Jane in her arms"—will stay with me
forever.

Sara Jane was still alive, but she never regained consciousness. Although she had serious internal injuries (which I only found out about later), she had no external injuries at all. She looked perfect. Her head had been shaved, and Zeb knew she would really be mad about that when she got home. But she never made it home.

As I lay in my own hospital bed, recuperating from injuries not nearly so serious, no one gave me any indication that Sara Jane might die. In fact, our family doctor told me she would be just fine. Of course, it never entered my mind that she would die, could die. That was an impossibility. No mother could ever believe that would happen.

Then on the fifth day after the accident, David, my husband, telephoned me from Sara Jane's room and said four words I'll never forget: "We're losing Sara Jane." She had had a brain seizure and there was no more hope at that point. Her brain was dead.

That afternoon, November 20, 1989, the three of us, David, Zeb, and I, gathered around Sara Jane's bed to tell her goodbye. Our lives took on a new course at that moment—one we knew nothing about, one that would change us forever. With our loss came grief and its constant presence.

My sisters and my mother had arrived at my bedside from the opposite coast within hours of the accident. Various friends met them at the airport, made sure they had a rental car and guided them to their already-reserved hotel rooms. My sisters became my bedside companions and when they weren't with me, they were at my new house putting my kitchen together. To this day, everything is still in the same place.

During my five-day hospital stay, many friends came to see me, but few got in, due to my sisters' vigilance. I remember Becky bringing me nourishing food and giving me a much needed and appreciated back rub and foot massage. There was a sign-in log at the nurse's station that I treasure to this day. Signatures and personal messages of hope and love were so nurturing to read during the long dark days and months that followed my daughter's death.

It is important to me that Sara Jane be remembered as the girl who lived—and who lived a loving life,—not as the girl who died. It is important to David, Zeb and me that we be known as the family who had a wonderful daughter and sister who we loved and who was a vital part of our lives, not as the family whose daughter and sister died. Keep this in mind as you comfort your friend. Through memories and love, their special person will always be a part of their lives. ∽

CHAPTER 1

HOW THIS BOOK
WILL HELP YOU

A few years before my 10-year-old daughter Sara Jane was killed in a car accident, my friend Valerie's daughter was hit by a car when crossing the street on the way to school. Several weeks later I saw Valerie for the first time since her daughter's death. "What in the world am I going to say?" was my first thought. Luckily, Valerie hadn't seen me. I quickly turned my shopping cart around and headed for the check out counter, even though I hadn't finished shopping. My own fear and lack of words made me unable to face her. I had no idea what to say, so I said nothing and successfully avoided her.

When Sara died I was able to see this same situation from the other side. My friend Karen lived in another town when Sara died, but I didn't hear a word from her for eight years. When we finally saw each other by chance, her first words, mixed with tears, were, "I'm so sorry I haven't called or written you. I just didn't know what to say." I could feel her grief and sorrow, not only for Sara, but for not reaching out to me years earlier. I understood completely how difficult it was for my very loving friend to respond to my grief. I had been there.

Have you ever had an experience when not knowing what to do or say has kept you from doing or saying anything, has kept you from comforting a grieving friend? You're not alone. In fact, you're in good company. Most people feel ill-equipped and awkward when faced with a friend's grief. We want to be supportive, but we just don't know how. And just as importantly, we are afraid of saying the wrong thing and making matters worse.

Our society doesn't provide us with much guidance on how to go to our neighbor's door when a loved one has died and say, "I'm here to help." Instead, we stay behind our own door, peeking out the window, when we really want to reach out. We just don't know what to do, so we turn away. We feel helpless and uncomfortable. Just imagine, however, if we feel this bad, how really horrible our grieving friend must feel. He doesn't know what to say or do either. Truthfully, our discomfort pales in comparison, so it is our loving responsibility to take the first step and reach out to our friend or neighbor.

■ THOSE OF US WHO HAVE LIVED THROUGH GRIEF KNOW FIRST HAND WHAT COMFORTS AND WHAT HURTS

There is a rewarding aspect in comforting your grieving friend. As you put aside your own fears and self-consciousness and put an arm around someone really in need, your fears will drop away and you will feel better about yourself. Everyone likes to know he has done something that makes a difference. The good news is that there are proven ways to help your friend experience healthy healing.

This book comes from my experiences as a grieving mother and from the suggestions of more than 100 people I interviewed, who have first-hand experience with the death of a loved one. Those of us who have lived through grief know what comforts and what hurts. We have a new understanding and a new awareness of the grieving process.

Each of us wants to provide tender care to our hurting friends, but we just don't know how. This book gives you the words, the actions and the confidence to connect and "be there" when your friend grieves and needs you the most. ∿

CHAPTER 2

IMMEDIATELY AFTER A DEATH

The afternoon of November 20, 1989, my husband David, our son Zeb, and I gathered around Sara Jane's bed to tell her goodbye. The unimaginable had happened. Sara had died. Our lives took on a new course at that moment—one we knew nothing about, one that would change us forever. With our loss came the constant presence of grief and the inability to think clearly or make a single decision.

PRACTICAL HELP

Our friends Steve and Maggie took us by the hand through the process of selecting a mortuary and a casket, making the calls to find four cemetery plots together, deciding where and when to hold the funeral and arranging for the musicians. Although our eyes were open and our feet were moving, David and I had no idea what needed to be done, much less how to do it. We couldn't have done it without them.

When a death occurs, whether it is anticipated or unexpected, people need immediate help. They need emotional support, hugs and kind words. They need good food and comfortable surroundings. They need practical aid in making a myriad of decisions. No matter how large or small a role you take, there is a place for you in the first few hours and days following a death. Perhaps you can meet family members arriving at airports, arrange lodging for out-of-town family and friends, see there is plenty to eat for arriving family, or tidy the house. Whatever you do, your friend will need your presence and appreciate your help.

Consider cultural, geographic, religious and social variations, that may not be the same as your own. Be attuned to these possible differences, but don't let them hold you back from helping. If you are unsure what to do or what will happen, ask. This will make you feel more at ease and less hesitant to help.

Grief takes a huge amount of energy. You can lift the load of everyday life so your friend can have the room and energy it takes to grieve completely. I can remember sitting in my living room knowing a lot was going on in the kitchen and dining room, but I wasn't able to do anything but sit. Flowers were delivered, food was dropped off, meals were prepared, dishes were washed and friends stopped by. The phone would ring and I couldn't answer it. It didn't matter. My friend Mary placed a notebook and several pens beside the phone and anyone who answered would write the messages down for me to look at later, when I was able. My wonderful family and friends kept my house running smoothly.

To help you at this difficult time, I have created two checklists. Both checklists appear at the end of this chapter and
at the end of the book. The first is a list of what needs
to be done immediately after a death. The second offers
suggestions for helping around the house in the early days.
Use these as a guide, since all situations are unique. The
lists are designed to help you make sure nothing is over-
looked. Make a photocopy to take with you.

The Quiet Time

In the first few hours following the death of a loved one,
emotions are intense and extreme, especially in the case
of a sudden, unexpected death. Raw agony, disbelief, con-
fusion, shock and anger are all likely to appear. They are
all normal, yet it is difficult to watch a dear friend in such
pain. Several years ago, David and I arrived at the home of
our friends and their two daughters a few hours after the
death of their eldest daughter in a car accident. One person was making a list of people to notify and had started
making the calls. Others began arriving with food and tissues, notebooks and pens. I started doing the dishes. We
did all this between holding our friends as they crumbled
and cried. We listened to them tell their horrible news
again to each new caller and watched the anger and grief
in their daughters.

After several more hours, there really wasn't much to

do. The food was on the table. The calls were made. Numbness had set in. It was a time of waiting, of just

being there. In some ways, it was an awkward time—just sitting and having small conversations with others who arrived. It was time for letting the grief sink in. With all the experience David and I had with death and grieving, we still felt inadequate. What should we be doing? What could we do? At this point, our presence was what we could offer, and our friends told us later that was all they needed.

There will be these moments, these uncomfortable, awkward times, when you can find no words or actions that feel helpful. Remember, it's okay to be quietly present. You don't have to make anything happen, worry about the checklist, or consider what the next phase will be. This is a time of stunned grief when the quiet can be essential. Allow that space to be there.

Anger and Humor

At some point, the anger just below the surface, the anger that is a natural part of the grieving process, may suddenly come out. After a drunk driver driving on the wrong side of the highway killed his son, Paul was insane with rage. He talked about finding the driver and shooting him. He paced the room in a frenzy, and no rational talk advising him against such an action could penetrate his fury. It took several days before Paul's intense anger gave way to grief and copious tears.

Paul's anger had a specific target, but the anger that comes with grief may pop up unprovoked and it may be aimed at you or another close person. If this anger comes at you, try to let it be there without making a negative response and without taking it personally. You are providing a safety zone for this rage to emerge. The anger will pass, and your friend probably will not remember the outburst.

Humor and laughter are the reverse side of anger. As family and friends gather, it may be the first time some of these people have met or seen each other in a while. They will talk about things unrelated to the grief around them. It's a reunion of sorts, and like most reunions, family and friends will recall old stories, talk about current events, catch up on careers and kids. It's pleasant to see each other in spite of the circumstances.

However, it's best to keep laughter outside the house, away from the grieving family. How can anything be funny? It's shocking enough to see the world going on as if noth-

▪ HUMOR AND LAUGHTER ARE THE REVERSE SIDE OF ANGER

ing has happened when their world has turned upside down. As we were leaving the cemetery after burying Sara Jane, I noticed a friend I had not seen in many years standing with a group. As we drove by unnoticed, I saw her throw her head back in laughter. She was talking with friends she hadn't seen in a long time and I know she was glad to see them. She meant no harm, but that vision still hurts me years later.

And yet it's true that laughter often appears side-by-side with grief. It's common for the grieving person to move from sobs to giggles. If you can, share that fleeting light moment. Laughter feels good and is therapeutic, but let your grieving friend set the tone.

Immediately After a Death Checklist

Here is a checklist of what needs to be done the first day or two following a death. How close you are to your friend and the family will determine which job you do, but there will be a place for you.

- Identify family members and friends to notify immediately by telephone. Divide the list with other friends who are there to help, then make the necessary calls. Provide a local contact number of someone other than the immediate family.

- Select and contact a funeral home. The funeral home will set up a time to meet with the family to determine the time and place for the service. Offer to accompany your friend to this meeting. Making decisions at this time of shock and stress is extremely difficult. Your friend will need your support and definitely should not drive.

- Make lodging arrangements for out-of-town family and friends. If there are enough friends offering to help, ask one person to be in charge of lodging.

- Arrange transportation from the airport for family members arriving from out-of-town.

- Help write the obituary. Funeral homes can provide direction. Include full name, age, date of death, cause of death (optional), names of surviving family members, names of close family members who have preceded this person in death, education, noteworthy achievements, hobbies, memberships in organizations. Conclude with date, time and place of service, and any request for memorials other than flowers. Will a picture accompany the obituary?

- Select and notify pallbearers.

- Ask if family members, including children, have the clothing they want to wear to the funeral. Help with needed shopping.

- If there are very young members of the family, suggest hiring a babysitter to stay with the child or children during the funeral. Help find one if needed.

- During the visitation, stay by your friend's side, providing physical and emotional support.

- Have water, tissues and chairs available for the immediate family.

- If the funeral home offers limousine service, encourage the family to use it. The family will appreciate being together. If this service is not provided, check into hiring a car service for the funeral, or ask friends to drive the family. This is not the time for them to be worrying about traffic, gas and parking. And grieving people should not be driving.

- If your friend must travel out-of-town to the funeral, offer to make travel arrangements, drive him to the airport and pick him up when he returns, feed the pets, pick up the mail, and generally keep an eye on things.

- If the deceased was living alone, notify utilities and landlord, and tell the post office where to send mail.

Help Around the House Checklist

The household needs taking care of, too. Your grieving friend will not be able to think about mundane tasks. You and others can keep the house running smoothly by doing the following:

- Pick up several spiral-bound notebooks, packs of pens, tissues, plastic eating utensils, paper plates and cups, and napkins, and bring them to the house.

- Answer the door and the telephone. Use a notebook to keep a record of all visitors and phone calls. Be sure to get the phone numbers of callers. Your friend will treasure this notebook later when he sees the support he received when he was in too much shock to appreciate it.

- Help make the house ready for visitors. Sweep the porch, wash the dishes, clear the dining room table for food, and set out plates, cups, utensils, and napkins in a convenient location. Make sure the bathrooms are clean and provide soap, toilet tissue and paper towels.

- Schedule food deliveries with neighbors and friends so there is always something wholesome and easy to eat. Several people interviewed mentioned how they appreciated "nibble" food, like cubes of cheese.

- Use disposable silverware and dishes to keep cleanup to a minimum. Ask visitors to label dishes they want returned, or to bring disposable serving dishes.

- Keep the kitchen organized and the dishes picked up and washed.

- Ask before undertaking a project that might seem too personal, like doing the laundry, or changing or disturbing anything that belonged to the deceased.

- Store the mail and newspapers in a container.

- Record who sent flowers, food and gifts in the note book. When flowers are delivered, write a brief description of the arrangement on the envelope. This will be helpful when writing thank you notes.

- Some people said they appreciated photos of the flowers that they could look at later. A disposable or digital camera is perfect for this.

CHAPTER 3

PLANNING THE RECEPTION

O ne of the few "rituals" we have in our culture is friends gathering together before or after a funeral or memorial service. This provides another opportunity for people to share stories and memories about the deceased. Most importantly, it is a time for friends to personally give their condolences to the family. Some grieving people don't want to have a reception because they think it will be too hard. They are right. But it will be much harder on them when people express their condolences individually when they see friends the first time over the next few years.

Donna and Paul were well known and loved by their many friends in their hometown. Their son Tom, 28, had moved to another city for college and stayed there after graduation. When he was killed in a car accident, they held the funeral two days later in his town, surrounded by his friends. It was too far and too soon for many of their friends to attend. When Donna and Paul returned home, Donna dreaded leaving her house for fear of seeing her friends and having to face their condolences and concern. She couldn't bear the thought of having to smile politely and say, "Thank you" over and over again. Her mother encouraged her to have a memorial reception in her hometown. She finally agreed, and was comforted by the outpouring of love and support her friends expressed. And it opened the door for those friends to help her in the following months and years.

My friend Cathy said she had always been a reluctant hostess. Her husband wanted to have parties, but she was never very eager. After her husband died, she wanted a reception for the 150 people who attended the memorial service. She had directions to her home available at the service and told everyone, "This is one time I can't say no."

But Cathy was in no shape to undertake such a big event in her own home. Anastasia, a good family friend, flew in from New York City, and I was there from North Carolina. Even though we didn't know the area, we took over. In one week we had the house cleaned from top to bottom by professionals, patio furniture refurbished with new cushions, caterers interviewed and hired, valet parking arranged, and the garden planted with new flowers.

At the same time, Anastasia and I kept Cathy's house stocked with food and beverages for the family and friends from out-of-town, as well as local friends. Many people delivered food. It was a week of 14-hour days for us, but it was what Cathy needed.

Help your friend decide what kind of reception to have. It can run from a simple gathering with punch and cookies, to a potluck with guests bringing a dish to share, to a festive "celebration of life" with catered food. In many communities, the women of the family's church prepare a meal for the family and close friends.

When arranging a reception in someone's home, you and other friends can take charge of the planning, shopping, setup, food preparation and cleanup. The basics to consider are food, beverages, plates, cups, utensils, napkins, extra chairs and tables, a guest book and plenty of parking. If everyone attending the funeral or memorial service is invited, provide directions and a contact phone number.

If the event is going to be at a restaurant or other public place, pay it a visit to make sure the space is what you are looking for. If appropriate, select the menu, décor, and flowers, and let the staff know approximately how many people will be attending.

CHAPTER 4

WHAT TO SAY
THAT IS HELPFUL AND KIND

A few days after my daughter Sara Jane died from a car accident, my friend Mary Jean came to see me. She came into our living room, sat down next to me on the couch, put her arms around me and cried. As we looked at each other, the anguish in her face and the tears streaming down her cheeks spoke more than any words she could have said. There was nothing to say, yet her actions spoke volumes about caring and compassion and love. It is one of the few moments that stands out in my mind during the blur of the first few weeks back home. No words were necessary.

A SIMPLE "I'M SORRY"

Granted, such demonstrative actions may not always be appropriate, or may not even be what you are feeling, but the point is not to rely too much on words to show your concern and caring. The most common concern of someone wanting to help a friend in a time of crisis is, "What do I say?" After interviewing scores of people who have been through heartbreaking times, I learned that the most appreciated words are simply "I'm so sorry." An acknowledgment of the tragedy, a willingness to address it, and a reaching out are the most helpful gestures, and, coinciden-tally, the simplest to do.

I always thought my words to a grieving friend needed to have a certain power, be meaningful and make everything better. I sincerely wanted to say the "right" thing, to be the one with the memorable words of wisdom to make the problem go away. I certainly didn't want to say the wrong thing. "What is the right thing to say? What are those magic words?" I continually asked myself.

The real question is: Can I really do or say anything that will make my friend feel good and make everything better? The answer is no. There are no magic words. We cannot make our grief-stricken friend feel good or take the pain away. It's important for us to let go of these unrealistic, self-imposed expectations that keep us from reaching out when we are so needed. Quite honestly, it's a huge relief to give up the pressure of needing to say just the right words at just the right time. Now, with that huge expecta-tion removed, what can you do? What is your role? Our role is to be a friend, not a counselor. Friends are there without being asked, to help do everyday things and to listen. It's as simple and as powerful as that.

▧ WHAT YOU SAY OR DO WILL DEPEND ON YOUR RELATIONSHIP WITH THE BEREAVED.

What you say or do will depend on your relationship with the bereaved. We had spent the Monday before our car accident moving into our new home. Sara Jane was thrilled to find it already had a microwave because we had never had one. As the afternoon wore on, the movers hadn't taken a break for lunch, so she decided we needed to feed them. Needless to say, we didn't have much in the way of food, but she found some blueberry muffins in the freezer. One of the men offered to teach her how to use the microwave. He spent quite a bit of time explaining all the buttons and options to her, and together they turned out perfect muffins for the whole crew. It was lovely to watch.

Several days after Sara Jane died, the doorbell rang and there was that kind man. His wife had driven him to our house because he was too devastated to drive. He asked simply, "Was it the same little girl?" When he heard yes, he just crumpled and said, "I'm sorry." He wouldn't come in and sit with us. He just turned away, his wife helping him to the car, and left. That "I'm sorry" will stay with me forever. His words were two of the most heartfelt and sincere of any spoken to us and had the most impact. I wish I could find him today to tell him how much I appreciated his caring.

It's okay to be honest and say, "I don't know what to say, but I'm here for you," or, "I don't have the words, they don't exist. I am here and I care." If you want to say more, add, "Would you like to talk about it? I'm here to listen." Or, like the kind man from the moving company, if all you can say is "I'm sorry," that's okay, too. Once you express your concern and show your willingness to be there, the conversation will take a natural course. What is most important is to be sincere and kind. Speak simply and from your heart.

Here is a list of suggested "starter" sentences to give you confidence when you don't know what to say.

1. "I cannot take away your pain, but I'll do what I can to help you."

2. "I can't imagine how you feel. Do you want to tell me?"

3. "I'm so sorry. I know this is never what you thought would happen. What a shock."

4. "It's okay to cry or be angry. You don't have to be strong. Do whatever you feel. I can handle it."

5. "I love you. You are in my heart." (Grieving people need all the reinforcement they can get.)

6. "He was a special person. We will all miss him. I remember the time... "

7. "We've been together in the good times. I'm still here for you now."

8. If you know your friend would appreciate it, offer to pray together.

9. "I'm sorry for your loss."

   [Sometimes saying more is worse, especially if the situation is complex, such as suicide or murder. You have opened the door to let your friend speak or say more if she wants to.]

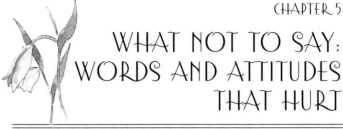

CHAPTER 5

WHAT NOT TO SAY: WORDS AND ATTITUDES THAT HURT

elen had spent many years caring for her 25-year-old son who had multiple sclerosis. She had taken a leave from work to be by his bedside continuously during his last month. Now, six weeks after his death, Helen went back to work. It was a difficult decision because she had heard from no one at the office. She knew how awkward and uncomfortable she and everyone else would feel. Her emotions were still raw, but at some point she would have to re-enter her business life. The time was now.

Everyone in the office was tense, but Helen pretended everything was fine. She plowed through a backlog of work. By the end of the week, she was emotionally exhausted. Her facade shattered. Sitting at her desk, she just started crying. Her boss happened in at that

> ▪ AS IMPORTANT AS KNOWING WHAT TO SAY IS KNOWING WHAT NOT TO SAY

moment, saw her head down and heard her sobs. His response: "Oh God, who died now?"

As shocking as this sounds, the story is true and not

uncommon. Most people are kind and well intentioned, but can be ignorant about grief. As a result, their actions and words can come across as uncaring or insensitive. They say things that only add to the pain, even when they mean well. As important as knowing what to say is knowing what NOT to say.

What words wounded or angered people when they were grieving? People gave me very specific examples when I talked with them. They explained why these phrases were so hurtful. Below is a list of comments actually made to people when they were hurting most.

DON'T SAY: "I know how you feel."

Even if you have had a similar experience, you can't know how someone else feels. Each person's reactions and feelings are completely unique. Each person has a personal relationship to the deceased, and the circumstances of a death are always different. Instead, try "I don't know how you feel, but I'm listening if you'd like to tell me." If you have had a similar experience, you could say, "I have an understanding of the pain and agony of grief, but I know your experience is different. Tell me how you feel. I'm here to listen."

DON'T SAY: "He's in a better place."

Even after Craig's long and difficult bout with prostate cancer ended with his death, his family still grieved for the loss of the person they loved. They may have been relieved that his suffering was over, and that they no longer had to tend him 24 hours a day, but these feelings will surface in the future. It may be "a better place" for the one who died, but for those grieving, he's gone and their grief hurts. You can say, "He was such a vital part of your family. I know you will miss him terribly."

DON'T SAY: "Things always happen for a reason."

Bereft people, regardless of their religious affiliation, often feel these clichés are ways of telling them to buck up. These sayings feel like justifications, creating a reason to end the conversation and the grieving. Leave these comments unsaid. People with strong religious faith may become angry with God and question their belief system at times of grief. Allow room for this reevaluation without judgment or advice. Let your friend find resolution in her own way, in her own time. Just listen and offer unconditional support.

DON'T SAY: "It could be worse."

Susan's 33-year-old daughter Beth drowned in a boating accident. At her funeral, a friend said, "At least now you don't have to worry about Beth ever

▓ JUST LISTEN AND OFFER UNCONDITIONAL SUPPORT

getting cancer, going through chemotherapy and having her hair fall out like me." Someone who could say this probably never experienced profound grief. These words convey no understanding, compassion or concern. Making comments like these is a good way to become a former friend.

DON'T SAY: "You should ..."

Friends can sometimes imply or insinuate that a grieving person "should" be doing this or that differently. It is not appropriate to tell a grieving person what they should or shouldn't do, even if you think you know best. We all have our ideas of what they should do, but it's not our call. If there is something you really want to recommend, such as getting outdoors in nature, offer it as a gentle, loving suggestion. Try "How about taking a little walk with me?" rather than "You should exercise." Instead of saying "Get out and do something," suggest "We'd like you to join us for dinner. We'll pick you up and bring you to our house. What sounds good that I can fix for you?" Remember to give your friend permission to opt out if she decides at the last minute that she just can't participate. Drop that dinner by her house and stay with her a little while.

DON'T SAY: "Aren't you over this yet?"

In the months following Elizabeth's mother death, she declined invitations from her many friends to join them for various activities. She was too sad and had no energy at all. She told me, "My friends want me to get over this. 'Enough already. Quit being so sad,' they say. They want to feel comfortable, so I have to get better for them."

"Aren't you over this yet?" implies that something is wrong

with the person who can't get over her grief. We have created artificial deadlines for grief—most commonly, one year. At the end of one year, people are supposed to be "back to normal" and "over it."

Grief doesn't work that way. It has no timetable. The process takes lots of twists and turns. In truth, it never ends. People just find a way of molding their everyday lives around the grief. Try not to push your friend. In fact, let your friend be your guide.

■ GRIEF...HAS
NO TIMETABLE

Each person will begin to heal at her own pace and in her own way, with almost as many steps backwards as forward.

Most people are uncomfortable with other people's grief. They don't want to see them in pain. It's agonizing to watch the sorrow of someone we care about. We truly want her to feel better. But pressuring our friend to stop grieving is an expression of our own personal discomfort, not what's best for her.

Crying and feeling sad are natural and essential parts of the grieving process. Encourage, not discourage, these feelings in your friend. (It can be very difficult to see our friends in such pain. If you find this to be true, take some time away from your friend to do your own grieving. Then return when you can be supportive and loving. It will make all the difference.)

If grief doesn't come out in healthy ways, in open tears

and anguish, it will hide in the body until it finds a more destructive exit, such as long-term anger and rage, depression, insomnia, or serious illness. This is a guarantee—grief will emerge. Instead of telling your friend to "pull it together and get over it," support the sadness. Be a shoulder to lean on.

Grief's intensity will lessen with time and become more manageable day-to-day, but the pain will never go away completely.

In the case of a stillbirth,
DON'T SAY: "Luckily it died before you had a chance to get attached."

Miscarriages and stillbirths are not properly recognized for the pain and grief they can cause. Just the awareness of pregnancy, not the length, creates attachment, love and dreams for the future.

■ HAVING OTHER LIVING CHILDREN IS A HUGE COMFORT These babies will always be "their children" to the people who conceived them. A simple "I'm so sorry for your loss" and some lovely flowers will mean a lot.

In the case of the death of a child,
DON'T SAY:"You're lucky to have another child."

This is a complicated statement. David and I were extremely fortunate to have our wonderful son Zeb still with us when Sara Jane died. It is so true that having other living children is a huge comfort and helps in the healing process. No doubt about it. But saying, "You're lucky to have another child" can be heard as dismissive. "You're okay. You have other children." Best to leave it unsaid.

Other words to avoid in this situation: "You'll have other children."

Every child is unique and loved. The surviving child or children do not make up for or take the place of the one who died, nor will a future child replace the one who died. Again, best left unsaid.

In the case of the death of a spouse,
DON'T SAY: "You're young. You'll get married again."

When Susan was 26, her husband was killed by a drunk driver in the first hour of their much anticipated two-week vacation. She was surprised so many friends told her, "You're young. You'll get married again." Susan said, "Tom was the love of my life, my perfect partner. Getting married again someday to somebody else is no consolation at all. I want Tom." Although the future may hold promise for us, the present is full of grief and loss for our friend. That's where we need to turn our attention, to help her grieve fully now.

DON'T SAY: "I didn't call because I didn't want to upset or remind you." Dr. Joyce Brothers says, "Don't ever hold back for fear of making your friend cry. Tears are an important part of the healing process." The truth is your friend is already upset and she hasn't forgotten. She will appreciate any expression of friendship and kindness, even if it starts tears. Not hearing from you compounds the pain and is worse.

Take a good look inside yourself, too. Are you not making that call because you don't want to upset your friend or because you are uncomfortable with facing her grief? Remember—no matter what you are feeling, your friend is feeling a lot worse. Your friend doesn't know what to say either. Reach out and give your support. The words will come.

Some people avoid a friend altogether, quickly heading down another aisle as I did in the grocery store when spotting Valerie in the store. Those in grief suffer when old friends never acknowledge their sorrow or loss, and just drop out of the picture. After a tragic loss, your friendship matters the most. Make that phone call, drop by for a visit, hold your friend's hand, and let her cry with someone familiar. If you can be there for the good times, be there for the bad times too.

DON'T SAY: "Let's talk about something else."

Once when I was visiting my mother a couple of years after my daughter Sara died, I noticed a new ceramic piece that played music when wound up. It was a kitten in a teacup. I wound it up and as it was turning I started crying. It was just the sort of doodad Sara would have loved because she adored cats. My mother became so upset when she saw my tears, she immediately put the toy in a drawer. Then she said, "Let's watch TV." I had to assure her it was okay for me to cry and that she had done nothing wrong. Talking about and thinking about Sara was something I wanted and needed to do and share with my mother.

■ GRIEVING PEOPLE NEED TO TELL THEIR STORY

Grieving people need to tell the story of their loved one over and over. It's a very important part of the grieving process. Our role as friends is to listen over and over again to the same tale. Pay attention, as if hearing it for the first time. When your friend doesn't need to tell the story anymore, he'll stop.

Often the suggestion to change the subject comes from a kind place. You're thinking, "Perhaps my friend will feel better, even if for a few minutes, if we talk about something else. I'll help lift the burden just a little." But to the one whose heart is broken, avoiding the loss, or quickly changing the subject, feels like a lack of interest, concern or caring. One of two things will then happen: your friend may stop telling the story, which is critical to her healing, or she will avoid you as a person to turn to in her time of need. Neither outcome is good. So take the time to listen. This is now her entire life, but it's a small part of your day. Ask: "Tell me about a favorite vacation you two had," and listen to the tale.

DON'T SAY: "You're so strong."

Rosemarie worked with the public every day at the bank. She

recalled, "If I heard how strong I was one more time, I was going to punch someone." Her son Leonard had died along with his best friend in a car accident. He was the second son she had buried: the first died of sickle cell anemia at the age of two.

Daily she had customers at the bank looking at her moon-eyed, telling her how they admired her and how strong she was. "Strong?" she said to me, "What in the world do they mean, strong? That I'm still alive? That I'm not in a loony bin? I'm barely getting by. I'm only here because I need a paycheck. Don't tell me I'm strong. One, it's meaningless, and two, who cares if you're strong? Anyone would trade strong for her child. I don't want to be any stronger."

In Rosemarie's story, being strong means being stoic, not crying, keeping emotions inside and going forward as if nothing had happened. But what does strong really mean? It means having the courage to face and experience the agony and anguish that grief brings, to feel the depths of despair, and to make the choice to survive as a healthy, albeit changed person. Stoicism puts off the hard work of grieving. Don't compliment or encourage your friend when she tries to be stoic. Encourage her to grieve, to cry, to show on the outside just how she feels inside.

As a friend, your role is to help, not hinder the grieving process. No artificial timetables, no stiff upper lip, no "let's talk about something else." Just be there and listen. Your friend will be forever grateful.

CHAPTER 6

WHAT MOST PEOPLE DON'T KNOW ABOUT GRIEF

Most people don't spend a whole lot of time thinking about grief. In fact the opposite is true. We avoid it at all costs. As a result, we don't know much about it. In my ignorance, I thought people were sad for a while, and then they got over their loss. Don't we give people three days off from work when a family member dies? It's been a year and you're still grieving? Get over it. It's only when grief is thrust upon us that we face it head on. That's when we begin the process of learning about grief, when we have no choice.

When I was interviewing bereaved people, I asked, "What do most people not know or realize about grief that you now know and want others to know?" Here is what they said.

GRIEF IS A SOLITARY EMOTION

I remember walking through the lobby of the hospital and driving through town on the way home after saying goodbye to Sara Jane. I remember watching

■ "I HAD NO IDEA WHAT GRIEF WAS REALLY LIKE. IT'S THE HARDEST WORK I'VE EVER DONE"

people have lunch in the cafeteria, honk their car horns, wait for the bus, go about their lives normally. My life stood still. It was like watching a movie through the car window. I felt completely alone, although I was surrounded by loving family and friends.

Grief is a solitary emotion. We know how to respond to joy. That comes naturally. We eagerly share the joy of a new baby, a marriage, a promotion, a new house. We can't wait to tell everyone our good news and we invite them in with smiles, hugs and tears of joy. As friends, our role is easy. Smile and be happy, too.

But grief works differently. When we grieve, we turn inward, remain private and shed tears of sadness. Our sadness is not inviting, and only those with an understanding of grief and the grieving process are brave enough to take a step toward us. It is not easy. Even those who have had grief in their own lives often feel inadequate in helping the newly bereaved. It never becomes easy because no two situations are ever the same.

GRIEF MAKES YOU CRAZY

My brother and sister-in-law Wayne and Susan came to our home shortly after Sara died. Wayne and I spent an afternoon sitting on the sofa talking. A number of years later I asked him about something and he looked at me like I was nuts. "Don't you remember? We talked about that when I was with you after Sara died." The answer was no, I don't

remember and yes, I was nuts...nuts with grief. I remember
him being there but I don't have a clue what we talked
about. Your friend may or not remember your presence,
but don't count on him remembering the conversation.
The brain is in a fog!

GRIEF IS HARD WORK

"I had no idea what grief was really like," said Susan not
long after her mother died. "My God, it's exhausting. It's
the hardest work I've ever done. I'm glad to get my teeth
brushed, my hair combed, and my clothes on. That's an
accomplishment. Thank goodness my friends are bringing
me food or I wouldn't eat at all."

Exhaustion is a side effect of grief that many don't know
about until it hits them directly. Everyday tasks become
monumental and anything requiring thought or concentration is overwhelming. Grief takes tremendous energy—
physically, mentally, and emotionally. Everything a friend
can do to help with daily chores helps the grieving person
make it through the day.

THE STORY NEEDS RETELLING

Robert's 17-year-old son Josh, a star football player on his
local high school team and the apple of his father's eye,
was always clowning around. One Friday after school before the big game that night, he was up to his usual hijinks
in the school parking lot: surfing on the hood of his friend's

car while the car was pulling out of the parking lot. Trying to stand on one foot, he lost his balance and fell off the hood, hitting his head on the curb. He died instantly.

Robert was devastated. Every time we saw him, he would tell us the story again. We would listen and ask him questions, until he moved on to another topic. Robert actually began speaking to high schoolers about the danger of car surfing, telling his story to prevent other teenagers from having the same accident. His healing came from using his experience—"telling his story" —to help other young people stay safe.

This is one way for grieving people to reach out of their solitary grief: tell their story. The telling is part of the healing process, making the tragic event real. Be there to listen when they tell their story again and again. Do the laundry, wash the car, LISTEN, address envelopes for thank-you cards, go to the market, LISTEN, pick up the kids, LISTEN. We think that recalling the story only brings up the pain, but there is a need to make sense of what happened, and telling the story helps the grief-stricken person do that. Ask questions, go into scary parts, don't be afraid. There's no need to respond with solutions or profound insights. You can't solve this. Just pay attention and listen.

GRIEF MAKES US STRONG AND VULNERABLE

Grieving people who are still on two feet and breathing are often referred to as "strong." Yes, in some ways they are stronger and yet, the opposite is also true. They are more vulnerable, too.

They are strong in that they have experienced the deepest pain and have survived. There is little that can touch them as deeply as the death of their loved one, so losses and difficulties that come their way now don't have the punch they once would have had. They pale by comparison and they can face them head on. In this way, they are stronger.

On the other hand, losing a loved one makes them more vulnerable, more attuned to the pain of others in the world around them. Since the pain is so close to the surface, it doesn't take much for bereaved people to feel tremendous empathy and compassion. They understand the pain and agony others are suffering when they see or read about their plights. The daily newspaper and the evening news frequently bring tears.

Grief Is Sneaky

Recently I found myself watching one of those bride reality shows on television. The bride-to-be was in a shop trying on gowns with her mother at her side. The young lady looked so beautiful and the mother was moved to tears. I found myself tearing up and crying, too. It was a scene I would never experience, and the power of that loss hit me hard and unexpectedly.

Bereaved people discover how unpredictable grief and

the pain that goes with it can be, how it can pop to the surface at any moment, even many years after the loss. Women who experience childbirth often say they would never have another baby if they could remember how much it hurt. They remember that it did hurt, but they can't feel the pain today.

With grief, the pain does come back, physically and viscerally, in every fiber of the body, a pain that is relived over and over, though less intensely as time passes. This wave of pain can be triggered unexpectedly, at any time, anywhere, by a certain song, a date on the calendar, a well-loved teddy bear, a young woman trying on a bridal gown. Grief is sneaky.

Even now, many years after the death of my daughter, when I see a mother and daughter shopping, riding side by side in a car, or having an ice cream cone and talking quietly to each other, my heart aches. I long to be hugging Sara Jane, laughing with her, deciding which flavors of ice cream to buy so we can share bites. I want to ask that mother and daughter if they know how lucky they are. I want to tell them to treasure these moments that appear so ordinary. That moment may be one of many that blur into the past, or it might be the last moment they'll have together.

The New Normal

Eight months had passed since Nancy's 11-year-old daughter died from a childhood illness.   Friends who had been attentive in the first days and weeks had drifted off one by one until she felt very alone. One night eating dinner out with her sister, she came across a table full of her friends. Stung by not being included, she tried to avoid them, but they spotted her and called her over. "We wanted to invite you," one friend said, "but we don't like the way you are now. We liked the old you, the way you used to be. When are you going to be back to normal?" Back to normal. Sounds like an obvious request, just give us a date and we'll call you then to join us again.

If normal means returning to how someone used to be before the death of the loved one, the answer is never. Never? Never is a mighty long time. But the answer is: never. Grieving people want this fact recognized. "I'll never be the same again."

Loss and the grief that follows causes changes that are permanent and indelible. During the initial grief period, the changes are obvious and show up in the anguished face, the defeated posture, frequent tears, red eyes, and the always handy box of tissues. There can be no doubt that this person is not the same as she was a short time ago. Something has changed.

As some of the external characteristics like laughter and

smiles reappear and the red eyes and easy tears fade, friends tend to think everything is back on track, back to normal. And in many ways, that's true. But this is a new person, a different person on the inside who has lived through a profound experience. We cannot expect him to ever be the same, to be back to the way he was before. He's changed.

As weeks, months and years pass and the external signs of grief become less obvious, it's easy to forget that the grief and its changes are still there. Now they are carried internally, making profound and permanent changes invisible to the outsider. A new normal has been created.

A new normal. That sounds like a contradiction, an oxymoron. But it's a very real truth. Someone or something held very dear is gone and grief has filled that void. Grief has moved in and taken up residence, never to leave. The initial anguish lessens and quietly subsides, but the ache, the void, the grief are always there, sometimes buried deeply, sometimes right on the surface.

The challenge is to recognize and accept that someone's grief is permanent, even when it's not obviously visible. No one "gets over" the loss of a loved one. "I've changed," said Tom, "but not for the worse. I'll never be the same person I once was. When my wife died, my dreams for the future died, too. Things that once seemed so important diminished. I now treasure every moment so much more. I appreciate life. I don't take it for granted. I have a new way of living, new priorities."

CHAPTER 7

THE
MEDICAL COMMUNITY

Rachel and Dean had eagerly awaited the birth of their first child and were finally in the delivery room. When Rachel delivered, the baby was stillborn. Their shock and grief were overwhelming. A short time later, when Dean and Rachel were in a private room mourning the death of their baby, the doctor came in and said, "Well, it seems we aren't having a very good day today, are we?" Rachel was too stunned to speak. Dean wanted to deck him. Instead he gathered their belongings and they left the hospital as fast as possible. Their pure grief was tainted with anger and rage because of an insensitive doctor and his thoughtless words. A simple "I'm so sorry" and a gentle touch would have meant so much. Dean and Rachel would have started on their journey of healthy grieving with support and caring.

The medical community, from first responders and emergency room staff to physicians

▪ THE NURSES HELPED MARTHA CREATE WARM AND LOVING MEMORIES BY CHOOSING TO BE KIND AND COMPASSIONATE

and nurses, has a unique opportunity. These professionals are often the first people family members encounter when a loved one dies or is dying. They set the tone for how we react at these most stressful and heartbreaking times. Kindness and consideration or rudeness and insensitivity are the choices caregivers have, and that choice will have a huge impact. If you work in the medical field, you can be efficient and considerate at the same time.

When Anne's husband Bernie needed urgent medical treatment and the paramedics arrived, they went straight to Bernie and began administering aid. Anne was standing at the side of the room, alone and paralyzed with fear. One of the paramedics noticed her. He put an arm around her reassuringly, telling her that they were doing everything they could and would take good care of him. Although still afraid and deeply worried, Anne was then able to get her wits together, gather up necessary paperwork and clothing, as Bernie was loaded into the ambulance for the hospital. The paramedic had considered Anne's feelings and needs, and by supporting her, too, made a most difficult time manageable for her.

Primary caregivers can make choices that support and help family members during end of life situations. When Martha's husband Johnny was in the hospital and dying, the nurses asked how they could help her. Martha said she would like to lie down beside her husband. The staff made that possible. They truly showed kindness and sensitivity both in asking about Martha's needs and fulfilling them so graciously. The nurses helped Martha create warm and loving memories by choosing to be kind and compassionate.

If you work in the health care community, take time to support the family members of the deceased. When everything else seems crazy, they will remember your sensitivity. Allow the family plenty of time to say good-bye in a private place. Even if the person who died was an adult, treat the parents with the same sensitivity you would show the parents of a small child. Age doesn't matter when your child dies.

CHAPTER 8

THE WORKPLACE: SUGGESTIONS FOR CO-WORKERS AND EMPLOYERS

Paul finally managed to get back to the office a few weeks after his wife of 28 years died of a sudden heart attack. It was all he could do to put on a suit and tie and a professional face when what he really wanted to do was curl up in bed and weep. How would his co-workers react? He found out. The first words out of his partner's mouth were, "How was your vacation?"

Granted, the workplace is often not made up of one's closest friends. Frequently we work side by side with people we hardly know, have a courteous relationship with them for eight hours a day, and that's it. But kindness, thoughtfulness and compassion can still prevail.

So what can really be expected at the workplace? Responses collected from bereaved people returning to work varied tremendously. Jack's assembly line co-workers offered to watch his machine

■ BE AS SENSITIVE TO YOUR EMPLOYEE AS YOU WOULD WANT SOMEONE TO BE TO YOU IF YOUR LOVED ONE HAD DIED

any time he needed to step outside or take a few minutes to be by himself. But Lance's buddies at the construction site ridiculed him and laughed every time he teared up remembering the birth of his stillborn son.

Avoidance or acting like nothing happened are also common reactions in the workplace, making the difficult task of returning to work even more painful, as well as confusing. "Do I act like nothing happened, too? Can I say my brother's name or talk about him? How am I supposed to act?" Danny worried. A kind acknowledgement, a hand on the shoulder and a warm smile go a long way to relieve any tension, and give your grieving friend permission to be honest and open with his feelings. "It's nice to have you back" is simple and warm. The only response that's needed from your friend is "Thank you."

A "Helpful Ideas for the Workplace" list is at the end of this chapter and at the back of the book. Adapt these ideas to your place of work or come up with ways that work best for your situation.

WHAT NOT TO DO

Carla's parents were killed in an airplane crash. She told me what happened when she returned to work. "Most of my co-workers avoided me. That really hurt, after working together for so many years. I don't expect them to be counselors, and many weren't close friends, but I observed lots of cold shoulders. People don't gravitate toward pain, but they leave you terribly lonely when they avoid you. Most co-workers can take a few minutes here and there to care and say they are sorry."

Arthur's co-workers not only avoided him when he returned to work, but they would talk behind his back or talk in whispers, thinking he didn't know what was going on. "That sixth sense is at work, making you especially sensitive and vulnerable. I knew exactly what was going on. It hurt and it made me mad. I'm not deaf and blind, just grieving."

To the Employer or Supervisor

It is understood that you have a business to run, deadlines to meet and obligations to fulfill. Yet a grieving employee may be experiencing a loss of concentration and impaired decision-making skills, plus memory loss. She may be tired all the time, depressed, withdrawn and completely lacking in confidence. Employers need to recognize that, to the newly bereaved person, the previous importance of her job has diminished. Nothing seems important compared to her loss. Your employee's mind is not 100 per cent on the job.

Most places of employment offer up to three leave days following the death of a family member. That's just long enough to get through the funeral. People are still in a state of shock and are numb during that time. The "real" grief doesn't set in until weeks or months later. How can this be accommodated at work?

For a few months, try to create a more flexible schedule and refrain from assigning new tasks that are too demanding or hazardous. Offer frequent breaks and a quiet place so your employee can have some alone time to cry, reflect or just collect his thoughts. Make instructions clear and be as specific as possible. Write them down so your employee has something to refer to when his mind wanders. Check in from time to time to see how he is doing and to lend your support. A pat on the back goes a long way.

Be careful not to treat your returning co-worker as if he were helpless. Being over solicitous can be annoying, too. Kindness, a warm smile and respect are what's needed. Your other employees will see what you're doing and follow suit, but you need to be the one to take the first step.

The most obvious rule to follow is also the most effective tool you have: Be as sensitive to your employee as you would want someone to be to you if your loved one had died. The employer who can provide a safe, understanding environment will undoubtedly have an appreciative employee who will become productive sooner and remain loyal longer. The kindness and compassion you show now will be greatly appreciated and will not be forgotten.

Helpful Ideas for the Workplace

Here are some helpful ideas and insights to ease the bereaved employee's transition back to work. Perhaps you and your co-workers can brainstorm more suggestions that are appropriate for your particular work environment. Your thoughtfulness will be appreciated.

- Expect your co-worker to have a short fuse, and don't take these outbursts personally.

- Understand that while your co-worker doesn't want to be excluded from the daily banter, he may not be able to join in with the laughter and fun for a while. Give him time and consideration.

- From time to time ask, "How are you doing?" and listen to the answer. It's always appropriate to express your concern, but a staff meeting may not be the time to delve into it. Suggest another time you might be able to get together, or talk on the phone in more depth. Then be sure and follow up.

- Since the grieving person's concentration is impaired, provide a notepad for your co-worker to write down what needs to be done.

- Invite your co-worker to have lunch with you and be ready to listen.

- Offer to help with some part of his job that you can do. Talk with your co-workers and figure out how you can work together to relieve stress for your work friend.

- If appropriate and needed, collect money to help with his expenses.

- Keep extra-soft tissues around.

- Business is not the same as usual. Remember that your co-worker is a different person now. Don't expect for him to be "back to normal," to be the same old pal.

- Avoid judgments of any kind. Instead ask how you can help.

CHAPTER 9

WRITING CARDS AND NOTES

C ards and notes are special because they can be opened and read when your friend is up to it and they can be re-read for months and years to come. I have a box full of cards sent to us when Sara Jane died and I go through them from time to time. The warm feelings expressed by my friends still comfort me today.

There are commercial sympathy cards available. If you find one with a message that expresses the sentiment you feel, then by all means send it. But make sure you add a personal note, perhaps "These words so beautifully express what I'm feeling for you." This little inscription will mean much more than just a signature.

You can write a note on a blank card, too. Select a card with a picture that is especially lovely or meaningful to you or your friend.

Now, what to say on that blank card. Again, there are no magic words to make everything better or stop the hurting. Keep your words simple and heartfelt. Your friend will read your words of sympathy and concern and know that you reached out. That's what matters.

The Right Words to Write

Finding those first words to write can be the most difficult. Below are some suggested openings. Use them directly or as a starting place to pen your own thoughts. Include your address, telephone number, and email address. Most grieving people find it impossible to pick up the phone or reach out at first, but when the day comes, your number will be handy. In the meantime, you can be the one to make contact initially. Your concern will always be appreciated.

- I am so sorry to hear about your loss. I'm here anytime, day or night, if you feel like talking. I'll call Thursday to see what you need.

- We send our sympathy and love. You are in our hearts. Please know we care.

- Please remember all the warmth and love you received from your Mother (Father)...I've felt it through you. (This can also be worded for the death of a child: "I know how much love you gave your son. I felt it in him.")

- Time will ease your sorrow, but we'll always have our memories of Mary.

- Our thoughts are with you. We hold you close to our hearts during this time.

- We are deeply saddened to learn of your loss. Be comforted by knowing you are in our thoughts and prayers.

- Just as we've been together in the good times, I'm here for you now in this most difficult time.

- I'm sorry I never met John. I hope you will tell me all about him when I see you.

- "I remember the time John..." If you knew the deceased, tell a special memory you have of him. It's nice to know how other lives were touched by our loved one.

- "One thing I always liked (admired) about John..."

CHAPTER 10

CARING FROM
A DISTANCE

When Sara Jane died, her former violin teacher Beth lived across the country in Montana. To honor Sara's memory, Beth gives free lessons to a violin student who wants to learn, but can't afford to pay. It is a lovely tribute that means so much to us—and Sara Jane wasn't even a good violin student!

We all move around so much these days that it's very possible you will be many miles away from a good friend when her loved one dies. There are still many ways you can show your concern and caring from a distance.

Think about what special thing you can do to honor your friend's loved one. Can you write a song or a poem, create a painting or a sculpture? Can you volunteer at a local school helping children read? Can you donate books to a library on a topic meaningful to your friend? Be creative!

> ▪ YOU CAN STAY IN TOUCH AND LET YOUR FRIEND KNOW YOU ARE THINKING OF HER WITHOUT BEING OBTRUSIVE

If the person who died was also a friend of yours, consider having a simple memorial service where you live. Plant a tree or other perennial in your own yard and tell your friend about it. Each year, send or email a picture of it as it grows, keeping the past in the present.

Here is a list of additional ideas. When you have the chance, plan a visit. There is nothing like a hug from a friend. This list is in the back of the book, too.

Caring From a Distance Suggestions

- Send flowers, if appropriate.

- Send a card with a few personal words, a treasured memory, or a photo of the loved one.

- Call on the telephone, but be prepared to leave a message. Don't expect a return call, but know your thoughtfulness is appreciated. Always leave your phone number, too. One day she'll be ready to talk with you, and your number will be handy.

Gifts are always welcome. Some suggestions are:

- Gift box with note cards, stamps and a nice pen for staying in touch with family.

- Gift box with unscented lotion, candle, gift certificate for massage, a day at the spa, or a favorite garden center.

- Blank book or journal with a personalized inscription.

- A book about grief. Your local bookstore can help you select one.

- Artwork that has special meaning to you or your friend. Decorate a picture frame with a special photo in it.

- Make a short movie of yourself or with family and friends, if your friend knows them, too. This is a wonderful way to personalize your feelings and give a gift that can be looked at over and over in the future.

- Make a donation in the deceased's name to your or your friend's favorite charity. Be sure and include your friend's address so she can be notified of the contribution.

With ever-changing technology, new ways for staying in touch are being developed every day. Email, texting, Facebook, twitter, Skype are all available now. You can stay in touch and let your friend know you are thinking of her, without being obtrusive. If you don't get a response, don't think the messages aren't being read. They mean a great deal, and she will reply when she's ready. And perhaps she won't reply at all. Your gift is a gesture of caring. No response is needed.

CHAPTER II

THE FIRST YEAR

I remember the first time after my daughter Sara died when someone asked me how many children I had. I was stunned. I didn't know how to answer. If I said one, then was I betraying Sara Jane? If I said two, did I need to say that one was dead? How was I going to answer that question the first time and from then on? And honestly, I don't remember how I replied that day, but that moment has stayed with me all these years.

My husband David is a musician who performs for audiences throughout the world. He remembers his first performance after our daughter's death. "The venue was in a nearby town in an auditorium with several hundred seats. I had decided I needed to play music for people to help me with my grief, as much as get back to work. I told the audience that my daughter had died a few weeks earlier in an automobile accident, and this was my first gig since then. It naturally made for a very quiet and attentive group, but the love and support that came from the audience during and after the concert has stayed with me all these years."

> THE FIRST YEAR AFTER THE DEATH OF A LOVED ONE IS THE HARDEST. IT IS A YEAR OF FIRSTS.

The first year after the death of a loved one is the hardest. It is a year of firsts. It will be the first year of having a birthday without the loved one there to join in the celebration. And it's also the first time to have her birthday arrive when she won't be there to grow a year older. It will be the first Mother's Day, first Father's Day, first day of school, first snow, first turning of leaves in autumn, first Thanksgiving, first Christmas or Hanukah, first beginning of the new year, first anniversary of the death, and many more less obvious first days in between. By the end of that first year, every holiday and "first" will have come and gone once.

Making the First Year Easier

How can you help make these firsts more manageable for your friend? Most importantly is to acknowledge and be supportive as these difficult days roll around. A simple email, note or phone call can let your friend know someone understands and is remembering along with her.

You can also offer to share the day or part of it by bringing over dinner, visiting the grave together, planting a new plant, sitting together looking at photos, and listening to whatever your friend has to say. Do what is comfortable for you or stretch yourself a little. It will be only a few hours for you, but it will mean the world to your friend.

On the one year anniversary of Sara Jane's death, Sandy and Dave brought us a special Dogwood tree, one that bloomed in June instead of April. June was Sara Jane's birth month. Every year, those beautiful white blossoms honor her and our thoughtful friends.

HOLIDAYS

Sara Jane died a few days before Thanksgiving. Many of our family members were in town from all over the country. Our friends the Hellers opened their home and included all of us in their Thanksgiving dinner with an ease and graciousness I'll never forget.

Christmas Day approached. Even though I had tried as hard as I could to keep things "normal" for our son, I just couldn't handle the thought of preparing Christmas dinner, and the three of us, not the four of us, sitting down and eating alone. Bett and her family opened their home with loving arms and shared their Christmas with us. It meant the world to us, yet I know it was very difficult for them, both physically and emotionally. I'm sure having our very sad family changed their usually festive event. But we were never made to feel unwelcome. In fact, we kept up our new tradition of having Christmas dinner at their house for many years. Bett's mother Molly was a vital and lively part of our Christmas celebration. The year she died, the thought of her empty chair was too much for all of us to bear. So the Christmas dinner was moved to our house after 10 years. It was a wonderful day with toasts to both Sara Jane and Molly at dinner.

For the big holidays, like Thanksgiving and religious celebrations, offer to do whatever it takes to make the day easier. Keeping the day exactly the way it always had been is what makes some people feel best. To others, a complete change is essential for maintaining sanity. But one thing is true: no matter how the day unfolds, it will not be the same as in the past. Loss has caused it to be different. Someone will be missing. Help your friend with whatever decisions need to be made. Remember how much energy grieving takes, and encourage your friend not to take on more than she can handle. Ask, "What do you want to do this holiday? What sounds and feels right to you?" Then help make that happen. Remind her that there is no "should" or "ought to," that she doesn't have to do anything she doesn't want to do. The first Christmas after two of his family members were killed, Mark was chided by his friend, who said, "You're going overboard with your grief by not having a Christmas tree and decorating it." It was Mark's call. There is no right way. He did what was comfortable for him.

Try to see the holidays through your friend's eyes. Not being able to shop for that perfect gift for the loved one who is gone; setting one less place at the table and that empty chair; hanging the Christmas stockings minus one; getting cards from friends that may not know; sending cards and letting friends know of the death. November and December can be very challenging months for someone so sad when everyone else is excited and happy.

If your friend's decision about how she would like to celebrate the holidays involves cooking, offer to take her to the market or do the shopping for her. Help get the china out and washed, decorations up, house tidied. Look around and do the little things that make a difference. How about fresh flowers or a special dessert?

Because of the unpredictable way grief works, if you have arranged to include your grieving friend in your holiday plans, understand that she may cancel at the last minute. Reassure her that that is fine and ask if there is something she would like instead that you can help with. Then follow through. It may change your holiday too, but helping will be the best gift you can give. It will make this holiday the most rewarding for you. Don't forget—a big plate of home cooking delivered in person is always welcome.

After the holidays, keep an eye on your friend because depression can set in. The energy required to get into the holiday spirit, attend holiday parties and gatherings, put on a cheerful face for others is exhausting. The person can crash once the festivities are over. A deeper grief and despair may ensue. Visit your friend several times immediately after a big holiday, share a meal, go for a walk, watch a movie, talk about holiday memories. This will help ease the transition back into the everyday world. A weekly phone call is always appreciated and serves as a good barometer to see how your friend is doing.

Ways to Help Throughout the First Year

There are many days throughout the first year after the death of a loved one that can be especially hard for your friend. The obvious days are the deceased's birthday, holidays and anniversaries. Other days may be more subtle, like your friend's birthday. Often the few days before an anniversary date or special day can be especially taxing, sometimes more than the actual day itself. Reach out a few days early to give support and friendship for the coming day. An Important Dates to Remember page is in the back of this book. You can fill it in with dates you know have special meaning to your friend as well as days that might be rough too, such as the first day of school if he lost a young child.

Remember birthdays and death dates with a phone call, email or note. To know someone else is remembering their loved one is tremendously comforting. As "big" holidays approach, invite your friend to share the holidays with you, or offer to help her decide whether to create a new tradition with new ways to celebrate, or to keep things exactly as they were. Remember: there is no right or wrong. Your role is not to judge your friend's decision, but to help make it a reality.

CHAPTER 12

IN THE FUTURE: HOLIDAYS AND ANNIVERSARY DATES

J ohn and Susan were caravanning in two cars across the United States to their new military post with their best friends Mark and Emily and their one-year-old son Eric. In the rear view mirror, John noticed that Mark's car was no longer behind theirs nor were any more cars coming down the highway. After a few minutes of waiting by the side of the road and seeing no more cars, John backed up to discover that Mark's car had run off the road and flipped over down an embankment. Mark and his wife had survived, but their son Eric had died. Earlier in the day

■ FOR THE PERSON IN PAIN, THERE IS NO RETURNING TO "NORMAL"

everyone had stopped for lunch and Eric had had his favorite meal—spaghetti. Now every year on the anniversary of Eric's birthday, the two families, though miles apart, eat spaghetti in Eric's memory. A lovely, simple way to honor this little boy.

As time goes by, our lives go back to normal. But for the person in pain, there is no returning to "normal." The grief remains, hopefully lessened, but nonetheless present every day. Life is still difficult and support is still needed. The year of firsts will pass, but every year thereafter, the same birthdays, death dates, anniversaries and holidays will happen again. Though the punch they pack will gradually lessen, these "special" days will always be there to be remembered and acknowledged.

It will mean a great deal to your friend if you call, email or send a note to let him know you are thinking of him on a challenging day. Every year I am amazed at the number of people who remember Sara Jane's death date. It truly is comforting to know she is remembered and that I am remembered, too.

Let your friend know you have not forgotten with a phone call, note or email simply to say, "I know Saturday is John's birthday. I want you to know I'm thinking of you and thought you might like someone to talk to. Would you like to get together for lunch or go for a walk soon?"

Second year holidays and anniversaries can often be worse than the first year because most friends will forget those important dates. Be the one to remember.

Reaching out can feel infinitely difficult. But if ▪ THROUGH MEMORIES AND LOVE, HIS SPECIAL PERSON WILL ALWAYS BE A PART OF HIS LIFE WELL INTO THE FUTURE you stop and think for one minute what a hard time your friend is having, it will seem easy for you to pick up a pen, make a call, or pay a visit.

73

CHAPTER 13

SOMETHING'S NOT RIGHT

eople show their grief in many ways. We all recognize tears, anguish, anger, fatigue, lessened memory and concentration, lack of appetite, sleeplessness or extra sleep. All of these traits and many more are part of the normal grieving process. But when any of these conditions become extreme, change dramatically, or last too long, it's important to pay attention and ask for professional advice. It may be a sign that something's not right, and that your friend needs professional help to move through her grief in a healing way.

Below is a brief list of behaviors that could indicate possible complications in the healthy grieving process. If you notice these or any other signals that could point to grief gone wrong, discuss it with your family doctor or a mental health professional. If he agrees there might be a problem, lovingly bring it to your friend's attention. If your friend doesn't see a problem, discuss it with a family member who may have more success getting the needed help. It will not be easy bringing up this topic with your friend or his family, but it is essential for healthy grief.

1. Extreme anger that includes threatening another person or threatening harm to himself.

2. Staying in bed for days at a time, months after the death occurred.

3. Lack of any emotion or acting overly positive, as if nothing had happened.

4. Excessive use of alcohol or drugs, including over-the-counter products.

5. Obsessively talking about, or totally ignoring speaking about the person who died.

6. Extreme changes in health.

Jeff, a friend of my husband David, called one day. His daughter had died from an illness a few months earlier. He asked David for some suggestions about how to handle the grief because he knew our daughter Sara Jane had died, too. After talking with Jeff, David realized he needed to write down what had helped him. Since then, his insights have proved helpful to other friends in grief. When the time feels right, give a copy to your friend to help her in the months and years to come.

CHAPTER 14

A ROADMAP FOR THE GRIEVING

by David Holt

Here are a few things that I think are important in dealing with grief of any kind. There is no easy way through it. You just have to walk through it as best you can. These are some things I have learned in the years since losing Sara Jane.

YOU ARE NOW ONBOARD THE RUNAWAY TRAIN CALLED GRIEF

You may feel semi-normal while you are in one of the passenger cars, but the train is carrying you down the tracks. There is nothing you can do about that because the energy that powers this engine is much stronger than any individual. It is a force of nature. You are going headlong into the future whether you like it or not. Moreover, this train has no engineer and can easily go out of control, jump the tracks, or crash. Your job is to steadily make your way to the engine and let off some of the steam so it can coast to a long, slow, safe stop.

Healing Is Not Linear But Moves in a Spiral

Few people realize that grief moves in a spiral motion and is not linear. Some days you'll be almost normal and the next day in deep dispair. Your mind will rest up to prepare for the next deeper step in the realization of loss. But the spiral is slowly moving upward toward healing and a new kind of "normal."

How Did You Survive?

Sometime, someone is going to ask you, "How did you make it though this awful loss? I don't think I could do it." The answer is simple: You live or you kill yourself. You have two choices here: Are you going to live out the rest of your life working towards a more creative, loving, healthy life? Or are you going to kill yourself quickly, or as often happens, kill yourself slowly with worry, anxiety, blame, guilt, and bitterness? It is actually a conscious choice you have to make everyday. If your choice is to do the best you can in this awful, unbelievable situation, then here are some of the things you need to do.

You Can't Handle It by Yourself

Some people think they can handle grief on their own. They are fooling themselves. It's like saying you can stand out in a raging tornado and not be affected, because grief is a force of nature, too. You are going to need all the help you can get and then some. Take it. Look for it. Build support into your life. When someone offers to help, say yes and tell them what you need. Your friends aren't mind readers. Tell them how they can help and let them take some of the day-to-day responsibility off your shoulders.

EVERYONE GRIEVES DIFFERENTLY

It is good to know this going in. I remember hearing about the couple who lost a child and the mother wanted to cover the walls with the child's photos. The father wanted all the pictures taken down and put away. Neither is "right." Some people can let it all out with crying and full emotion. Some feel the need to control themselves and hold the emotions in. Some get angry, some get quiet and withdrawn. There is no right way to do it (although holding it in does seem to have negative long-term affects on your health). Give people lots of space for their style of grieving. Ask them to give you the same.

ANGER IS A NATURAL BY-PRODUCT OF GRIEF

With emotional turmoil swirling inside everyone affected by the loss, there is bound to be anger. It can come out in a million different ways. But rest assured, the emotions are going to come out one way or another. Some people are much more comfortable with anger than with crying. Anger allows you to focus and to place blame. It allows you to concentrate on something other than the person who died. You are going to see lots of anger in yourself and others. Know that it is just part of the terrible storm. Let it pass. Don't dwell on it. It will pass.

Read Everything You Can About Grief

Lots of good books have been written about grief and its stages. Read them.

Only those who have experienced deep grief know what you are going through. While every situation is different, there are experiences that are common to most grieving people. You can learn from these and prepare yourself for what is about to come your way. There is a little war going on inside you. Grief is a natural healing process, but if you don't help it heal you, it will kill you.

Walk

I didn't say exercise—I said, walk. Just get up, get out the door and walk. Of course, the thing you want to do most is curl up in the fetal position and never wake up, but you need to get outside and move. Start slowly. Perhaps just go through the motions, or if possible, for the pleasure of just walking. Work up to an hour a day or more. If you start slowly, each time your body will heat up and you will begin to move with more vigor as the walk progresses. Build a daily walk into your life for the rest of your life. It is one of the best things you can do for yourself. When a friend asks, "What can I do?," ask them to walk with you.

OBSERVE NATURE

Nature has many subtle things to teach us about birth, life, and death—things that cannot be expressed in words. Being in nature teaches us not to be bitter, that life and death exist together all around us.

GIVE YOURSELF LOTS OF TIME TO REST

You will be addled and forgetful. Your mind won't work properly for a long time, but it will come back to functioning properly. Go easy on yourself. Don't take on projects or extra duties. Let others help you.

GET RID OF STRESS

Your body is under tremendous stress right now and will be for a number of years. It is time to start yoga classes or some such activity. Walking will help a lot and yoga will help you move forward, stay focused and get stronger.

Grieving Takes a Lot of Energy

You won't be able to keep your former schedule for a while. Slow down, don't expect too much from yourself or your family. You will get tired easily. Rest when you do. Grief also takes your focus and your memory. One of the most common side effects among grieving people is the inability to remember anything. Recognize this and don't be hard on yourself when you lose your train of thought or forget something frequently. You're in good company.

It Will Never Be the Same

Your life will never be as it was. You will never "get over it," but you will heal. You will laugh again. You will be creative and will enjoy life again. But now, you must find a safe place for the pain you feel. And the only way to do that is to travel through the grieving process successfully. You can't get around it. Know that you can never make things the way they were. You won't be "back to normal" as much as your friends will want you to be. You will find a "new normal" that incorporates grief as an integral part of your being. In time you will find a place for the hole in your heart. You're not the same. Something as powerful as experiencing the loss of a loved one changes you, but if you allow yourself to grieve openly and honestly, the change will not be for the worse.

GET COUNSELING

A really sensitive, intuitive counselor is invaluable, and I think, indispensable. Don't worry about people thinking you are crazy. You have just gone through the worst a human can endure and that makes you a little crazy. Your world is turned upside down. You need help. Get it. If you try and lock the feelings away, they will eat you alive.

JOIN COMPASSIONATE FRIENDS OR A SIMILAR SUPPORT GROUP

If you are a parent whose child has died, Compassionate Friends is a valuable resource. While the meetings can sometimes be undeniably painful, you are with a group of people who deeply understand what you are going through. You can learn and express a lot with them. Most importantly, one day you will find yourself helping some new member of the group and realize you just turned a major corner in your grief.

EAT WELL

You have to take care of yourself in every way possible. Eat clean, healthy food, lots of green vegetables—you know, the good stuff. Stay away from liquor and drugs. They only make things worse. Your body needs to stay strong to handle the punches grief is giving it. Keep it healthy and you'll do much better and heal faster.

Again if someone wants to help, ask them to bring "real food" in from time to time.

THINGS WILL GET BETTER

It may seem difficult to believe now, but time will heal you. If you really work at getting better, you will come out of this a wounded but much deeper, compassionate and life-loving person. You will find a place for this pain that seems overpowering now. You will actually experience profound joy again.

On a personal note, I have been pondering a question I don't know the answer to: Must we personally experience tragedy and grief before we change our life's priorities, before we "stop and smell the roses" on a daily basis?

Survivors of natural disasters, train wrecks, house fires, wars and violent crimes often look at life differently. They feel changed. They say they are going to enjoy that second cup of coffee with their family in the morning, spend more time doing fun things with their kids, not sweat the small stuff. They see how precious life is and how fleeting life can be. They are shaken from complacency, jolted from looking at life as humdrum, and are ready to put the joys of their lives first, not second or third or last. They are literally going to stop and smell the roses.

It took their lives being turned upside down for this shift in priorities to happen. Again, my question is: Must this be the case? Is there any way we can take time to enjoy our families, nature, and special moments on a daily basis without being traumatized first?

I have asked many people, from all walks of life this question. All but one person has concurred that it takes a powerful and traumatic event for us to bring the beauty and value of life back into our daily routine. Who was that one person with a different response and what did he say?

Who was the one person who told me, "Yes, we can have the right priorities without living through trauma and grief first"? It was a Buddhist monk. He told me that we all *know* the important things in life, but we don't *choose* to take the time to stop for five minutes and watch the sunset, or tell our child or spouse that we love them, or add a candle to the dinner table. Quite honestly, what he said was, "We are lazy."

We all know how hard it is to break a bad habit like smoking, or to start a new discipline, like exercising. It's hard work and it takes a conscious effort, but when we set our mind to it, we can do it. We want to create a change, so that the change becomes a priority. The same is true about looking at life differently. It may take great effort initially, but if we consciously make it our goal to notice and appreciate small moments in life, then the pattern will set in and become part of our lifestyle.

My good friend and master storyteller Jay O'Callahan tells a wonderful story about a young boy who has this sense of what is important without even knowing it.

Brian is a seven-year old-boy who lives in the north-west of America. He's a bit of a dreamer, so he got in trouble in school a lot. One day his mother got a call. It was Brian's teacher. She was furious.

"I'm calling because Brian was one hour late for school. Now, I'm not going to put up with this kind of thing. You know he's a dreamer. One hour late." The teacher was so angry, she just hung up. When Brian got home that afternoon, his mother said, "Brian, what happened?"

"Teacher was really mad today. I was an hour late."

"I know, Brian. She called me. Why were you an hour late?"

"Well, it must have rained last night because the worms were all over the sidewalk and I knew the kids would step on them after school. So I had to put them all back. Took an hour."

His mother bent down and said, "I love you, Brian."

※ ※ ※

Everyday we have the opportunity to enjoy these gifts of life all around us. Let's make that our new priority before tragedy happens to us for the first time or again. We will not regret missed opportunities, and our lives will be fuller.

RESOURCES TO OFFER YOUR GRIEVING FRIEND

One of the best books for a grieving person is **How to Go on Living When Someone You Love Dies,** by Therese Rando, 1988, Bantam Books.

Also excellent is **Healing and Growing Through Grief,** by Donna O'Toole, M.A., available from Compassion Books (see below).

You can find an entire catalog of grief books covering a wide variety of topics for people of all ages from Compassion Books, 477 Hannah Branch Rd, Burnsville, NC 28714. Phone (828) 675-5909.

www.compassionbooks.com

Compassionate Friends is an organization for parents whose children have died. There are local chapters throughout the country. You can contact them for a chapter near you.

The Compassionate Friends, Inc.

Toll-free: (877) 969-0010

PH: (630) 990-0010

www.compassionatefriends.org

GriefShare offers grief recovery support groups throughout the US and Canada.

GriefShare

PO Box 1739

Wake Forest, NC 27588

Phone: 800-395-5755

International: 919-562-2112

info@griefshare.org

www.griefshare.org

www.helpguide.org/topics/grief.htm has a helpful section on coping with grief and loss.

The Hospice Foundation has a wonderful section on grief on its website, as well as information about how to find local grief support groups.

www.hospicefoundation.org

GriefNet.org is an Internet community of persons dealing with grief, death, and major loss. GriefNet. org has almost 50 e-mail support groups and two web sites. Their integrated approach to on-line grief support provides help to people working through loss and grief issues of many kinds.

www.griefnet.org

Immediately After a Death Checklist

Here is a checklist of what needs to be done the first day or two following a death. How close you are to your friend and the family will determine which job you do, but there will be a place for you.

- Identify family members and friends to notify immediately by telephone. Divide the list with other friends who are there to help, then make the necessary calls. Provide a local contact number of someone other than the immediate family.

- Select and contact a funeral home. The funeral home will set up a time to meet with the family to determine the time and place for the service. Offer to accompany your friend to this meeting. Making decisions at this time of shock and stress is extremely difficult. Your friend will need your support and definitely should not drive.

- Make lodging arrangements for out-of-town family and friends. If there are enough friends offering to help, ask one person to be in charge of lodging.

- Arrange transportation from the airport for family members arriving from out-of-town.

- Help write the obituary. Funeral homes can provide direction. Include full name, age, date of death, cause of death (optional), names of surviving family members, names of close family members who have preceded this person in death, education, noteworthy achievements, hobbies, memberships in organizations. Conclude with date, time and place of service and any request for memorials other than flowers. Will a picture accompany the obituary?

- Select and notify pallbearers, if needed.

- Ask if family members, including children, have the clothing they want to wear to the funeral. Help with needed shopping.

- If there are very young members of the family, suggest hiring a babysitter to stay with the child or children during the funeral. Help find one if needed.

- During the visitation, stay by your friend's side, providing physical and emotional support.

- Have water, tissues and chairs available for the immediate family.

- If the funeral home offers limousine service, encourage the family to use it. The family will appreciate being together. If this service is not provided, check into hiring a car service for the funeral or ask friends to drive the family. This is not the time for them to be worrying about traffic, gas and parking. And grieving people should not be driving.

- If your friend must travel out-of-town to the funeral, offer to make travel arrangements, drive him to the airport and pick him up when he returns, feed the pets, pickup the mail, and generally keep an eye on things.

- If the deceased was living alone, notify utilities and landlord and tell post office where to send mail.

- NOTES:

Help Around the House Checklist

The household needs taking care of, too. Your grieving friend will not be able to think about mundane tasks. You and others can keep the house running smoothly by doing the following:

- Pick up several spiral-bound notebooks, packs of pens, tissues, plastic eating utensils, paper plates and cups, napkins and bring them to the house.

- Answer the door and the telephone. Use a note book to keep a record of all visitors and phone calls. Be sure to get the phone numbers of callers. Your friend will treasure this notebook later when he sees the support he received when he was in too much shock to appreciate it.

- Help make the house ready for visitors, sweep the porch, wash the dishes, clear the dining room table for food, set out plates, cups, utensils, and napkins in a convenient location, make sure the bathrooms are clean and have soap, toilet tissue and paper towels.

- Schedule food deliveries with neighbors and friends so there is always something wholesome and easy to eat. Several people interviewed mentioned how they appreciated "nibble" food, like cubes of cheese that were easy to eat.

- Use disposable silverware and dishes to keep clean up to a minimum. Ask everyone to label dishes they want returned or bring disposable serving dishes.

- Keep the kitchen organized and dishes picked up and washed.

- Ask before undertaking a project that might seem too personal, like doing the laundry or changing anything that belonged to the deceased.

- Find a container to hold the mail and newspapers.

- Record who sent flowers, food and gifts in the notebook. When flowers are delivered, write a brief description of the arrangement on the envelope. This will be helpful when writing thank you notes.

- Some people said they appreciated photos of the flowers that they could look at later. A disposable or digital camera is perfect for this.

Suggestions for talking with your bereft friend

1. "I cannot take away your pain, but I'll do what I can to help you."

2. "I can't imagine how you feel. Do you want to tell me?"

3. "I'm so sorry. I know this is never what you thought would happen. What a shock."

4. "It's okay to cry or be angry. You don't have to be strong. Do whatever you feel. I can handle it."

5. "I love you. You are in my heart."
(Grieving people need all the reinforcement they can get.)

6. "He was a special person. We will all miss him. I remember the time"

7. "We've been together in the good times. I'm still here for you now."

8. If you know your friend would appreciate it, offer to pray together.

9. "I'm sorry for your loss." Sometimes saying more is worse, especially if the situation is complex, such as suicide or murder. You have opened the door to let your friend speak or say more if he wants to.

Helpful Ideas for the Workplace

Here are some helpful ideas to ease the transition back to work. Perhaps you and your co-workers can brainstorm even more ideas that are appropriate for your particular work environment. Your thoughtfulness will be appreciated.

- Expect a short fuse and don't take outbursts personally

- Understand that while your co-worker doesn't want to be excluded from the daily banter, he may not be able to join in with the laughter and fun for a while. Give him time and consideration.

- From time to time ask, "How are you doing?" and listen to the answer. It's always appropriate to express your concern, but at a staff meeting may not be the time to delve into it. Suggest another time you might be able to get together or talk on the phone in more depth. Then be sure and follow up.

- Since concentration is impaired, provide a notepad for your friend to write down what needs to be done.

- Invite your co-worker to have lunch with you and be ready to listen.

- Offer to help with some part of the job that you can do. Talk with your co-workers and figure out how you can work together to relieve stress for your friend.

- If appropriate and needed, collect money to help with expenses.

- Keep extra-soft tissues around.

- Business is not the same as usual.   Remember that your co-worker is a different person now. Don't expect for him to be "back to normal," to be the same old pal.

- Avoid judgments of any kind. Instead ask how you can help.

Caring From a Distance Suggestions

- Send flowers, if appropriate.

- Send a card with a few personal words, a treasured memory, or a photo of the loved one.

- Call on the telephone, but be prepared to leave a message. Don't expect a return call, but know your thoughtfulness is appreciated. Always leave your phone number, too. One day she'll be ready to talk with you, and your number will be handy.

Gifts are always welcome. Some suggestions are:

- Gift box with note cards, stamps and a nice pen for staying in touch with family.

- Gift box with unscented lotion, candle, gift certificate for massage, a day at the spa, or a favorite garden center.

- Blank book or journal with a personalized inscription.

- A book about grief. Your local bookstore can help you select one.

- Artwork that has special meaning to you or your friend. Decorate a picture frame with a special photo in it.

- Make a short movie of yourself or with family and friends, if your friend knows them, too. This is a wonderful way to personalize your feelings and give a gift that can be looked at over and over in the future.

- Make a donation in the deceased's name to your or your friend's favorite charity. Be sure and include your friend's address so she can be notified of the contribution.

With ever-changing technology, new ways for staying in touch are being developed every day. Email, texting, Facebook, twitter, Skype are all available now. You can stay in touch and let your friend know you are thinking of her, without being obtrusive. If you don't get a response, don't think the messages aren't being read. They mean a great deal, and she will reply when she's ready. And perhaps she won't reply at all. Your gift is a gesture of caring. No response is needed.

Important Dates to Remember

Circle these dates on your calendar and remember your friend with a card, phone call, email, flowers or a visit. Let her know you haven't forgotten.

Friend's name

Address

Home phone (   )

Cell phone (   )

Email

Name of deceased loved one

Birthday

Death date

Additional occasions and dates with special meaning: (e.g., wedding anniversary)

1.

2.

3.

Days that might be especially difficult: (e.g., first day of school, Mother's Day, Father's Day, religious holidays, Thanksgiving)

Acknowledgements

It took me years to write this book. My sister Myra actually planted the seed the day I came home from the hospital after telling my daughter Sara Jane good-bye. As she tearfully tucked me in bed, she said, "One day you'll write about this." I don't remember what I replied, but I remember her nodding, saying, "Yes, you will."

Thank you to The Writers' Workshop of Asheville, NC for offering workshops for new and experienced writers. Each class gave me the encouragement and constructive guidance I needed.

As the chapters evolved, many friends, writers and editors read and critiqued them. My heartfelt thanks to all of you. Your insights and suggestions kept me going.

Thank you to the many people I interviewed for telling me your positive and your painful memories. Your stories are the core of this book.

A loving thank you to Jay O'Callahan who gave me permission to use his tender story 'Brian.' Check out all of Jay's terrific stories at www.ocallahan.com.

A very special thank you to Dana Irwin who designed this book with skill, artistry and patience. In addition to her layout skills, she drew a lovely native North Carolina wild flower to decorate each chapter. Dana, you made my dream a reality.

My son Zeb and Pablo Picasso were the inspirations for the cover design. Dana arranged the wild flowers from each chapter into a beautiful bouquet for the cover.

I am honored to say I have too many kind and caring friends who supported David, Zeb and me than I can list. I hope you know how much we depended and still depend on you. Thank you is not enough, but thank you.

I'd love to hear your experiences while helping your grieving friend—what worked, what didn't, a new idea, a unique situation. Email me at highwindy@gmail.com or visit www.afriendingrief.com to post a comment or ask a question. You can order additional copies of the book for your friends at that website, too. Become a friend of A Friend in Grief on facebook.

About the Author

Ginny Callaway was moved to write *A Friend in Grief: Simple Ways to Help* after her ten-year-old daughter, Sara Jane, died in an auto accident.
Meeting with other grieving people in support groups, Ginny heard upsetting stories of insensitive, hurtful comments made by well-meaning friends, family members, co-workers and others. This inspired her to write a guide to help friends navigate these difficult times with more understanding and thoughtfulness.

Although this is her first book, Ginny's career has been in communication. She is the founder of High Windy Audio, an independent record label featuring children's music, storytelling, and traditional folk music. Her proudest professional achievement is receiving a Grammy Award as producer for Stellaluna.

Ginny and her husband David Holt, a multi-Grammy Award winning musician, television host and entertainer, live halfway up a mountain near Asheville, North Carolina with a calico cat and a neighborhood family of black bears. The couple's son Zeb Holt lives in New York City.

CPSIA information can be obtained at www.ICGtesting.com
Printed in the USA
BVOW011906051111

275353BV00004B/1/P